The Ancient Text of the New Testament

The Ancient Text of the New Testament

by

DR. JAKOB VAN BRUGGEN

Professor of New Testament
at the
Theological College
of the
Reformed Churches in The Netherlands

(Broederweg, Kampen)

PREMIER PUBLISHING
WINNIPEG

Bruggen, Jakob van, 1936 —
The ancient text of the New Testament

Translation of De tekst van het Nieuwe Testament.
Translated by C. Kleijn.

ISBN 0-88756-005-9
ISBN 90-6015-328-6 (Dutch ed.)

1. Bible. N.T. — Criticism, Textual —
Addresses, essays, lectures. I. Title.
BS2325.B7813 225'.4'8 C76-016021-X

A translation of
DE TEKST VAN HET NIEUWE TESTAMENT
[Kamper Bijdragen XVI]
Publisher: "DE VUURBAAK," Groningen 1976)

1ST PRINTING 1976
2ND PRINTING1979
3RD PRINTING 1983
4TH PRINTING 1988
5TH PRINTING 1994
6TH PRINTING 1997
7TH PRINTING 2002

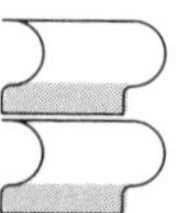

PREMIER PRINTING LTD.

ONE BEGHIN AVENUE, WINNIPEG, MANITOBA, CANADA R2J 3X5

Preface

On December 8, 1975, I delivered a lecture on the text of the New Testament at the anniversary of the Theological College at Kampen. This lecture has been published in the Dutch language by the 'Vuurbaak' in Groningen as volume 16 of the series 'Kamper bijdragen'. Mr. C. Kleijn was so kind to translate it into English.

Kampen
February 1976.

J. van Bruggen

Contents

The Last Certainty of New Testament Textual Criticism

The New Testament textual criticism of the twentieth century is characterized by great uncertainty. On the surface the opposite seems to be the case. Since the start of this century, in Protestant circles people have already united themselves around the text of Nestle. This agreement concerning the text that must be followed with Bible-translation and exegesis, appears to be becoming even greater in the next decades. A Greek basic-text has been edited for the United Bible Societies by an international team of textual critics. This text will serve as basis for all the translations of the Bible in the coming years. It will also be printed in the newly set up 26th edition of Nestle. Not only for Protestant circles, but also for Catholic biblical scholarship, this text will in future form the basis. Thus it seems that internationally and interconfessionally the greatest possible agreement will be attained in the twentieth century[1].

All this does not yet mean that there is certainty about the correct text of the New Testament. Agreement can be based on mutual certainty, but also on mutual uncertainty. And the latter is the case. The text of Nestle was not drawn up at the time as a best possible copy of the original text. Eberhard Nestle did nothing more than give an edition in which one could find the mean of some modern text-editions: Tischendorf, Westcott-Hort and Weiss[2]. It appears from the Einführung which Nestle wrote, that he personally still saw many unanswered questions[3]. He also tended to attach much greater value to the so-called Western text, than is apparent in his text-edition[4]. This same Nestle, besides his well-known mean-text, also took care of the fourth impression of Scriveners edition

[1] In 1966 the first edition of *The United Bible Societies' Greek New Testament* appeared. See R.P. Markham, E.A. Nida, *An Introduction to the Bible Societies' Greek New Testament*. New York 1966. Carlo M. Martini also worked on the preparation of the following editions, besides the members of the original committee: Kurt Aland, Matthew Black, Bruce M. Metzger, Allen Wikgren. J.K. Elliott gave a lengthy review of the 2nd edition (1968) in *Novum Testamentum* 15 (1973) pp. 278-300. The definitive text will appear in the 3rd edition, which is expected in 1976. This will be similar to the text of Nestle-Aland in the 26th edition. See *Bericht der Stiftung zur Förderung der neutestamentlichen Textforschung für die Jahre 1970 und 1971*. Münster 1972, pp. 41-43. Information about the 26th edition of Nestle-Aland in *Bericht der Stiftung zur Förderung der neutestamentlichen Textforschung für die Jahre 1972 bis 1974*. Münster 1974, pp.19-35.

[2] In the first two editions Nestle followed the edition of Weymouth (1886), besides Tischendorf and Westcott-Hort. Since the third edition this was exchanged for the edition of Weiss (1894-1900).

[3] E. Nestle, *Einführung in das Griechische Neue Testament*. Göttingen ^{3}1909, p. 246: ". . . nur freilich, dass ich jetzt weniger als je in der Lage bin, positive Vorschlage zu machen, auf welchem Wege das Ziel der nt. lichen Textkritik zu erreichen sei".

[4] E. Nestle, *Einführung in das Griechische Neue Testament*. Göttingen ^{3}1909, pp. 240-249.

of the Stephanus-text of 1550: a form of the so-called textus receptus[5]. It was certainly not intended by Nestle that his well-known text should become a sort of standard for the 20th century. Yet this is what happened. And that mainly because, as yet, nobody after Nestle has been able to show convincingly which text would have to be followed as definitive. For lack of growing certainty, the tentative edition of Nestle continued to dominate the field[6].

In the sixties of this century it was hoped that this situation could soon be changed. Yet it became more evident all the time that this expectation could not easily be fulfilled. The initial plan of Aland to offer a new, scientifically determined text in the 26th edition of Nestle, has been abandoned[7]. This 26th edition will give a revised text-critical apparatus, but it will present the text that has been determined for the 3rd edition of the Greek New Testament published by the United Bible Societies. This again means an acquiescence in a consensus-text which has been determined on the basis of *un*certainty. This time no mean from three modern text-*editions*, like the older Nestle, but the mean of the opinions of five modern textual-*critics*. Aland, Black, Martini, Metzger, Wikgren together have established a text by majority-vote. It is clear from the Textual Commentary of Metzger on this text, that there are many readings which have been chosen only by the *majority* of the committee[8]. That they did not unanimously arrive at a text, is also not surprising. At present there is no certainty concerning the history of the textual tradition[9]. In modern textu-

[5] F.H.A. Scrivener, *Novum Testamentum textus Stephanici A.D. 1550, cum variis lectionibus editionum Bezae, Elzeviri, Lachmanni, Tischendorfii, Tregellesii, Westcott-Hortii, versionis Anglicanae emendatorum*. Cambridge ³1891. In 1906 the "Editio quarta ab Eb. Nestle correcta" appeared (reprint in 1916).

[6] For history and location of the Nestle-text, compare K. Aland, Der heutige Text des griechischen Neuen Testaments. Ein kritischer Bericht uber seine modernen Ausgaben. (K. Aland, *Studien zur Uberlieferung des Neuen Testaments und seines Textes.* [Arbeiten zur neutestamentlichen Textforschung II]. Berlin 1967, pp. 58-80).

[7] For the initial plans, see the article of Aland, mentioned in the preceding note, pp. 77-79.

[8] J.K. Elliott, The United Bible Societies' textual commentary evaluated (*Novum Testamentum* 17 [1975] pp. 130-150), concludes: "This therefore is by no means a text based on unanimous decisions but is to a very large extent a text created by compromise. Such is the main danger of committee work!" (p. 136). Elliott also points out that the lack of agreement often influenced the use of the "rating system" for "readings": ". . . we see that many of the readings labelled C or D where we might have expected A or B are labelled in this way not necessarily to pass judgment on the text *per se* but to show that the committee was not unanimous. Like the use of square brackets, a C or D rating is often a sign of compromise." (pp. 137-138).

[9] Reviews on the modern textual criticism can be found among others in the following works: B.M. Metzger, *The Text of the New Testament. Its Transmission, Corruption, and Restoration*. Oxford ²1968. J. Duplacy, *Où en est la critique textuelle du Nouveau Testament?* Paris 1959. J. Schmid, Der Text des Neuen Testaments (A. Wikenhauser, J. Schmid, *Einleitung in das Neue Testament*. Freiburg ⁶1973, pp. 65-186). J.N. Birdsall, The New Testament Text (P.R. Ackroyd, C.F. Evans [eds], *The Cambridge History of the Bible. Volume I: From the Beginnings to Jerome.* Cambridge 1970, pp. 308-377). F.G. Kenyon, *The Text of the Greek Bible*. Third Edition Revised and Augmented by A.W. Adams. London 1975.

al criticism the eclectic method is generally followed: per *reading* a decision is made on the basis of a complicated structure of considerations. Subjectivity is not out of question with this method. Thus they will just have to arrive at a text by majority-vote. Nobody is happy with this. However nobody also dares to state that there is already sufficient certainty to do it differently. Thus the agreement concerning the text-*edition* to be used camouflages the uncertainty which prevails during the *fixation* of the text. It is no wonder then that Epp, in a recent retrospection of the last century of New Testament textual criticism, speaks dismally about an interlude without real progress[10].

Among all uncertainties of this 20th century, we, however, can point to one great, lasting *certainty* in the modern textual criticism — a certainty that serves as startingpoint and keeps stimulating much conscientious work and constant research. One can even say that the modern textual criticism of the New Testament is based on the one fundamental conviction that the true text of the New Testament is at least *not* found in the great majority of the manuscripts. The text which the Greek church has read for more than 1000 years, and which the churches of the Reformation have followed for centuries in their Bible translations, is now with certainty regarded as defective and deficient: a text to be rejected. This negative certainty has grown in the 18th century since Mill, Bentley, Wettstein, Semler and Griesbach[11]. It has found expression in text-editions of the 19th century[12]. From the close of that century until now, it has become visible for the Bible-reading community: in 1881 the Revised Version in England no longer followed the current Greek text and in the 20th century the same applies for new translations in other countries. The churches are becoming aware that the text of centuries is replaced by the text of yesterday: the Nestle text.

This rejection of the traditional text, that is the text preserved and handed down in the churches, is hardly written or thought about any more in the 20th century: it is a fait accompli. To hear the arguments for this rejection one must go back to the 19th century, back to the archives. Our century is accustomed to the disregard of the text that is indicated with names such as: Byzantine, Antiochene, Koine, Syrian or Ecclesiastic-

[10] E.J. Epp, The twentieth century Interlude in New Testament Textual Criticism. (The W.H.P. Hatch Memorial Lecture). *Journal of Biblical Literature* 93 (1974) pp. 386-414.

[11] J.I. Doedes gave a detailed assessment of this period in, *Verhandeling over de tekstkritiek des Nieuwen Verbonds.* (Verhandelingen rakende de natuurlijke en geopenbaarde Godsdienst, uitgegeven door Teyler's Godgeleerd Genootschap XXXIV). Haarlem 1844, pp. 74-240.

[12] Karl Lachmann's edition of a Greek New Testament (1831) paved the way for other editions that also abandon the textus receptus. Earlier editions with a text composed independently, continued to have little effect (Daniel Mace [1729]; William Bowyer [1763]; Edward Harwood [1776]).

al[13]. Already for more than 100 years the certainty that this type of text is inferior has been taken for granted. Yet certainty about a better, superior text-type has failed to come during this long time. The heritage of the 19th century criticism was a *solitary* certainty — the certainty of the inferiority of this "traditional text". And it remains to be seen whether the 20th century will have a new, second certainty to offer as a heritage of its own.

That still very little progress has in fact been made, despite much intensive work, is apparent from the procedures followed to prepare new scientific editions of the Greek New Testament. The editors of the International Greek New Testament are of the opinion that for the time being one must still print the rejected textus receptus as the basic text. Only at a later stage it will then be possible on the basis of the scientific apparatus to produce a substituting and better text[14]. The Germans have for decades already opposed this procedure[15]. Aland also refuses to make a compromise at this point[16]. Under his leadership preparations are being made for the Editio Critica Maior, which will offer a text that will ultimately be determined by Aland himself on the basis of the textual material[17]. However also for Aland the first step on this road is a confrontation with the Byzantine text. With the aid of his institute at Münster he tries to set aside and dismiss all the Byzantine material. A system of 1000 passages must serve to determine whether a manuscript can be typified as "byzantine". First of all 85-90% of all the manuscript material is in this manner put aside as inferior and then the remaining 10-15% can be worked

[13] None of these names satisfy as a description of the text-form that became generally accepted in the course of the church history. In future a number of these descriptions will therefore be used alternately, without preference for one particular term. Thus with "Byzantine text", "Church text", or "traditional text" we understand the same type of text. Terminologically, we distinguish the mentioned names from the name "textus receptus", which is used to describe the printed form of the traditional text from the 16th and 17th century.

[14] Information on this project can be found in *New Testament Studies* 16 (1969-70) pp. 180-182.

[15] In 1926 E. von Dobschütz writes in connection with an English plan to publish a scientific Greek text of the New Testament: "Wenn aber die Entscheidung der Engländer für den textus receptus ausfallen sollte, so würden wir darin die Aufforderung erblicken, eine eigene Ausgabe neben die englische zu stellen, ungeachtet der auch von uns anerkannten Bedenken gegen eine solche Doppelarbeit.". Von Dobschütz writes on behalf of the Neutestamentlertagung at Breslau (1926) that they as Germans are of the opinion that it is an "unerträglicher Anachronismus" to take the textus receptus as basis for collation of manuscripts as long as no other text has scientifically been determined. (*Zeitschrift für die neutestamentliche Wissenschaft* 25 [1926] p. 318).

[16] Cf. K. Aland, Bemerkungen zu Probeseiten einer grossen kritischen Ausgabe des Neuen Testaments. (K. Aland, *Studien zur Uberlieferung des Neuen Testaments und seines Textes*. [Arbeiten zur neutestamentlichen Textforschung II]. Berlin 1967, pp. 81-90).

[17] Cf. K. Aland, Novi Testamenti Graeci Editio Maior Critica. Der gegenwärtige Stand der Arbeit an einer neuen grossen kritischen Ausgabe des Neuen Testamentes (*New Testament Studies* 16 [1969-70] pp. 163-177).

on intensively[18]. It is still uncertain how the remaining data must be *evaluated*[19]. Yet people already start from the one certainty, that the Byzantine text which is found in most manuscripts is unimportant.

It is striking how emotionally people often speak about this one certainty. The textus receptus, which stands very close to the Byzantine text, is considered a "tyrant" that finally "died a slow death"[20]. Sometimes it seems as though a certain frustration about the continual absence of certainty concerning the right text of the New Testament leads to aggressive statements about the old certainty of the textus receptus. It is striking how Epp in his earlier-mentioned retrospection leaves room for many questions and uncertainties, yet suddenly speaks very denigratingly about some people who in the 20th century have dared to make positive statements concerning the textus receptus[21]. It is strange that in the realm of modern textual criticism all types of searchers and sceptics are given a place, but that those who revert to a former certainty are disqualified as renegades.

This friction between certainty and uncertainty in modern New Testament textual criticism gives occasion to ask what reasons are given for rejecting the Byzantine or Church text, which has been used for so many centuries. After a century of less encouraging experiences on a new road, it is useful to look back to the intersection at which one turned off from an old road. In science the investigation of the arguments should always receive a legitimate place. True science does not depend on the authority of a few experts or the tradition of generations. Even though it is appar-

[18] See K. Aland, Die Konsequenzen der neueren Handschriftenfunde für die neutestamentliche Textkritik. (K. Aland, *Studien zur Uberlieferung des Neuen Testaments und seines Textes*. [Arbeiten zur neutestamentlichen Textforschung II]. Berlin 1967, pp. 180-201, esp. pp. 194-196). In addition *Berichte der Stiftung zur Förderung der neutestamentlichen Textforschung* 1969, pp. 36-37; 1970/1, pp. 21-24; 1972/4, pp. 43-44 (Münster 1970 resp. 1972 and 1974).

[19] See the article of Aland mentioned in the preceding note, p. 196.

[20] F.G. Kenyon, *Recent Developments in the Textual Criticism of the Greek Bible.* London 1933, writes about the situation after the fall of the textus receptus: "But it has sometimes happened in history that when a victory has been won, the allied victors fall out over the spoil; and so it has happened here." (p. 10). Yet at the same time Kenyon remarks: "It would serve no good purpose to exhume the dead or to re-slay the slain." (p. 8). E.J. Epp writes in *Journal of Biblical Literature* 93 (1974) about "the final overthrow of the tyrannical textus receptus" (p. 386), while he simultaneously complains about "the diffuse, indeterminate, and eclectic NT textual criticism of our own present and recent past" (p. 387). G. Zuntz, *The Text of the Epistles. A Disquisition upon the Corpus Paulinum*. London 1953, writes: "The Textus Receptus died an undeservedly slow death." (p. 7). But Zuntz at the same time considers the modern text-editions to have arrived at a "deadlock" (p. 8).

[21] Epp's remarks are made in connection with the books of E.F. Hills, *The King James Version Defended! A Christian View of the New Testament Manuscripts*. Des Moines 1956; D.O. Fuller, *True or False? The Westcott-Hort Textual Theory Examined.* Grand Rapids 1973. These writers condemn the rejection of the Byzantine text, which the textus receptus followed. Epp then writes: "I suspect that no one of us will or need take these books seriously, but that they could be written at all and published in our own day is, in a way, an indictment of our discipline." (*Journal of Biblical Literature* 93 [1974] p. 405).

ently sufficient for many exegetes to note that "most scholars" or "modern textual criticism" reject the church text, we must agree with the modern textual criticism that the majority *in itself* is not decisive. Not the majority of manuscripts, but the weight decides. That also applies in a different way: not the majority of scholars in a particular century, but the weight of their arguments decides. In this case it is particularly important to test the arguments, because here the translation and explanation of God's Word is at stake[22]. Translators of the Bible and exegetes will notice the consequences of their choice in favour of a certain text-edition[23]. Translator and exegete deal with the *how* of translation and exegesis, but the text-edition decides *what* is to be translated and explained. Here respect for the Word of our God compels us to be very careful. We must be able to account for our treatment of the text that has been handed down to us. There is a scientific and a religious duty to ask the question whether the ancient text of the New Testament is *not* found in the majority of the manuscripts and whether the church has failed to follow the truly *ancient* text for many centuries.

A critical investigation of the reasons for rejecting the Byzantine text soon encounters the difficulty that this rejection is accepted as a fact in the 20th century, but not defended as a proposition. For the argumentation one is usually just referred to the work of Hort in the 19th century. Yet various arguments of Hort are no longer generally accepted today. People have learned to think differentiatingly about his reasoning from the conflate readings. Opinions are divided about the existence of a recension by Lucianus. Therefore one can not say that the reasoning of Hort is without question the reasoning of the 20th century textual criticism. On the other hand no new, supplementary arguments against the Byzantine text have been worked out. Therefore, it is in fact still possible to do justice to the various argumentations since Hort implicitly via a confrontation with the total reasoning of Hort himself. Hort developed his view on the text that he called "Syrian" in a broad treatise on textual criticism in general[24]. For our purpose it is, therefore, more convenient to arrange the arguments materially rather than to follow these in the order in which

[22] Hermann Kunst writes: "Denn auch die in den grossen Kirchen heute gebrauchten Ubersetzungen, selbst wenn sie ein ganz modernes Entstehungsdatum aufweisen, werden die Änderungen berücksichtigen müssen, welche der neue Text enthält, und zwar mit allen Konsequenzen, die das mit sich bringt." (!) (*Bericht der Stiftung zur Förderung der neutestamentlichen Textforschung für das Jahr 1969*. Münster 1970, p. 27).

[23] B.B. Warfield, *Counterfeit Miracles*, reprinted Edinburgh p. 167, weakens the defence against faith healers by accepting that Mark 16:17-18 are "spurious". F.F. Bruce, *I and II Corinthians* (New Century Bible) London 1971, p. 115, can relate I Corinthians 11:29 to "the corporate unity of all who share his life" because he does not consider the words τοῦ κυρίου to be original. N.B. Stonehouse, The elders and the living beings (in: *Arcana Revelata.* Kampen 1951, pp. 135-148), can only regard the 24 elders in Revelation as angelic beings because with the Alexandrinus he omits ἡμᾶς in Revelation 5:9.

[24] *The New Testament in the original Greek. The Text revised by Brooke Foss Westcott and Fenton John Anthony Hort*. Vol. II: Introduction (pp. 1-324). Cambridge 1881.

Hort offered them. His gradually developed view on the Syrian text, which forms the frame for all later reasoning against the traditional text, can be summarized as follows:

1. this text goes back to a revision of the Greek text in the 4th century, probably under the leadership of Lucianus of Antioch;[25]
2. this text can on external grounds be characterized as a late text: it is not found in the old majuscules and it is not followed by the Church Fathers before Nicea in their New Testament quotations;[26]
3. this text can on internal grounds be characterized as secondary because of its inclusive nature (conflate readings) and because of its tendency to harmonize and assimilate, leading to a complete and lucid text[27].

These arguments seem so strong, that it appears to be rather superfluous to bring them into discussion again after 100 years. On the other hand, it must be remembered that for centuries people could daily acquaint themselves with the character of the Byzantine text or the textus receptus, yet they did not regard this as secondary and inferior. One should also consider that the Church Fathers were known and read at least just as well in previous centuries as at present, whereas no occasion was found in the patristic quotations of the New Testament to suspect the age of the current Greek text of the New Testament. Certain things always remain puzzling. If Hort's arguments are proven right, then it is strange that they were not advanced earlier. If they are wrong, the question becomes urgent why they were still generally accepted in the last century. However, at the moment we will not try to give an explanation for this puzzling phenomenon, but we will concentrate our attention on the question what force the arguments of Hort *in themselves* have. After all, on the ground of *these* arguments people were so bold to abandon the traditional text. The latter did not occur on the ground of newly found papyri. The papyri only begin to play a part in the New Testament textual criticism in the middle of the 20th century[28]. The textus receptus was then already abandoned. Many people who use the Bible think that the Bible translations had to be altered with regard to their text because of the discoveries in Egyptian sand. Yet the reality is different. The Revised Version dates from 1881. In the practice of Bible-translation and exegesis, the Byzantine text was already abandoned decades before important New Testament papyri were published. Whether or not the new discov-

[25] Op. cit. pp. 137-139.

[26] Op. cit. pp. 107-115; 148-152.

[27] Op. cit. pp. 93-107; 115-119; 132-135.

[28] A quite recent survey of the papyri can be found in K. Aland, Das Neue Testament auf Papyrus. (*Studien zur Überlieferung des Neuen Testaments und seines Textes*. [Arbeiten zur neutestamentlichen Textforschung II]. Berlin 1967, pp. 91-136). Compare in this same volume pp. 137-172 and 181-191.

eries support the arguments of Hort is a separate question[29]. We can deal with this question separately later on. Yet, historically, it should stand in the perspective of rejection of the traditional text, which took place in the last century on the ground of arguments systematized by *Hort*.

[29] Pessimistic is the opinion of J.N. Birdsall, *The Bodmer Papyrus of the Gospel of John*. London 1960, pp. 8-9: ". . . the terminology and textual history based by Hort and his predecessors upon the manuscript evidence available to them is not fitted to describe or explain the earlier evidence which has since come to light." Optimistic is the opinion of G.D. Fee: ". . . the point of wonder is not that we still follow Westcott and Hort, but that they, without our discoveries and advances, revealed such remarkable judgements." (P^{75}, P^{66}, and Origen: the Myth of early textual Recension in Alexandria. In: R.N. Longenecker, M.C. Tenney [eds.], *New Dimensions in New Testament Study*. Grand Rapids 1974, pp. 19-45, esp. p. 45).

The Value of the Number of Manuscripts

The Byzantine textual tradition, which is at present rejected, is found in a large majority of manuscripts. Rightly so Aland introduces the new siglum 𝔐 (Majority-text) for this text-type. When the team of textual scholars, that determined the Greek text for the United Bible Societies, could not come to an agreement, the opinion of the majority settled the matter. Seeing that there is still no certainty in the 20th century about the correct text of the New Testament, one could consider allowing the majority of manuscripts to decide the matter. Why does not this happen? Because, according to most people, this majority of manuscripts can be traced back to one recension: the many manuscripts would be nothing else than copies of only one manuscript. The large number is traced back to the one recension in the 4th century. The majority is reduced to a minority which receives only one vote and then also only a secondary vote because here we are thought to have a later revision of the original and not a faithful copy of it. In this way, the large number is reduced and disqualified. The counted majority appears to be a weighed minority. Two matters call for attention here. In the first place, the question whether historical proof can be given for the proposition that the text of the New Testament has undergone a revision in the fourth century. In the second place, the question whether the Byzantine textual tradition can be characterized as the result of such a recension.

The historical starting-point for this recension-idea is sought in the person of Lucianus of Antioch[30]. That we, however, can not speak with great certainty here, appears from the fact that Hort did not do anything more than mention the possibility that Lucianus stands at the beginning of the Byzantine text[31]. In the sixties of this century Metzger still refers to what he calls the decisive work of Lucianus[32], but it is striking that he does not repeat this name in his later *Textual Commentary*. Metzger then still speaks only about "the framers of this text"[33]. It is also not possible to prove historically that Lucianus of Antioch offered a revised text of the *New* Testament. Even though for a long time, since De Lagarde, people

[30] Lucianus of Antioch died in 312 A.D. His life and work is completely treated by G. Bardy, *Recherches sur saint Lucien d'Antioche et son école*. Paris 1936.

[31] Hort, *Introduction* pp. 138-139.

[32] B.M. Metzger, The Lucianic Recension of the Greek Bible (*Chapters in the History of New Testament Textual Criticism*. [New Testament Tools and Studies IV]. Leiden 1963, pp. 1-41).

[33] B.M. Metzger, *A Textual Commentary on the Greek New Testament*. London 1971, p. xx.

have anxiously searched for the assumed LXX-recension of Lucianus, some are at present even sceptical concerning Lucianus' revisionary work on the *Old* Testament[34]. What Hieronymus says in mutual contradictory statements about the work of Lucianus, also gives little support[35]. In any case there is no clear indication in Hieronymus' statements of influential work that Lucianus was thought to have done on the Greek *New* Testament[36]. If he was busy with a revision of this text, his work remained of very limited value[37]. This also appears to be so from the fact that the later *Decretum Gelasianum* speaks with aversion about some Lucianic manuscripts[38]. If the original Greek text is superseded by an inferior recension in the 4th and following centuries, then this process has left surprisingly few trails behind in the historiography. Does this point out that people

[34] H. Dörrie, Zur Geschichte der Septuaginta im Jahrhundert Konstantins (*Zeitschrift für die neutestamentliche Wissenschaft* 39 [1940] pp. 57-110). D. Barthélemy, *Les devanciers d'Aquila*. (Supplements to Vetus Testamentum X). Leiden 1963. As opposed to Barthélemy, S. Jellicoe continues to plead for the idea of a recension of the LXX by Lucian (*The Septuagint and Modern Study*. Oxford 1968, pp. 157-171; 346-348).

[35] A biographical note in *De Viris illustribus* (*MSL* 23,723) mentions that some Bible-editions stand in Lucian's name till in the time of Hiëronymus. (". . ut usque nunc quaedam exemplaria Scripturarum Lucianea nuncupentur"). The influence of these editions seems great: in the *Prologus in Libro Paralipomenon* (Vulgata, ed. Weber, Stuttgart 1969, I p. 546) Hiëronymus writes: "Constantinopolis usque Antiochiam Luciani martyris exemplaria probat". This remark, however, only concerns the Old Testament and it is weakened in the letter to Sunnia and Fretela (*Epistula CVI*; *CSEL* 55,248). There Hiëronymus remarks that the version of the Greek Old Testament (to be distinguished from the original LXX), which was commonly spread for a long time, received the name *Lucianea* at a later date. On the other hand, Hiëronymus in his *Praefatio in Evangelio* (Vulgata, ed. Weber, Stuttgart 1969, II p. 1515) again does speak about emendation of the Greek Old Testament by Hesychius and Lucianus. Perhaps this passage should be interpreted in such a way that Hiëronymus now places in the name of Hesychius and Lucianus an emendation of the original LXX-text, which had already taken place some time ago in what he called the Koine text of the Greek Old Testament; he does this because the ancient text, which he considers to be a corrupt text, was later known under their name in Egypt, Syria and surroundings respectively, and because they too, therefore, took upon themselves the responsibility for these emendations when they gave their support to the time-honoured Koine-text of the Greek Old Testament.

[36] Influence on the *New* Testament is only mentioned by Hieronymus explicitly in his *Praefatio in Evangelio*. There he minimalizes the extent of that influence: "Praetermitto eos codices quos a Luciano et Hesychio nuncupatos paucorum hominum adserit perversa contentio". There is reason to suppose that Lucian's work on the New Testament mainly consisted in additions to the text already set apart as canonical. We italicize certain words in the following quotation: ". . . cum multarum gentium linguis Scriptura ante translata doceat falsa esse quae *addita* sunt. Igitur haec praesens praefatiuncula pollicetur *quattuor tantum* evangelia . . . ." Both in the light of the older Greek manuscripts to which Hieronymus himself goes back, and in the light of translations that went back to inferior manuscripts, we can establish that Lucian *added* to the New Testament.

[37] H. Dörrie, *op. cit.* pp. 70-87, gives a broad discussion on later information derived from liturgical and hagiographical sources: he concludes that nearly all this information is tendentious and must be explained from the desire to be able to appeal to an other authority overagainst the authority of Origenes in a later conflict about the correct text of the Old Testament.

[38] "Evangelia quae falsavit Lucianus apocrypha; evangelia quae falsavit Isicius apocrypha" (E. von Dobschütz, *Das Decretum Gelasianum de libris recipiendis et non recipiendis, im kritischen Text herausgegeben und untersucht*. [Texte und Untersuchungen 38, 4.] Leipzig

were never aware of such a process? Or does this show that such a process did not take place? These questions can only be answered by going into the second point that calls for attention here: can the Byzantine text be characterized as a recension on the basis of its textual tradition?

Although the name of Lucianus is mentioned less and less as the historical starting-point, people in the 20th century maintain with undiminished certainty that there was a recension in the 4th century. This is striking. Closer examination of the Byzantine tradition has shown, in the period after Hort, that several tendencies can be pointed out in this tradition. Von Soden distinguished various layers in these Koine manuscripts[39]. It proved to be impossible to describe the layers as a variation arising within a group of manuscripts, which in fact all go back to one archetype. That there is much agreement between all these manuscripts does not mean that they all come from one and the same source. The later research-work done by Lake and Colwell did change the picture given by Von Soden, but at the same time it has shown even more clearly that it is better to describe the Byzantine textual tradition as a collection of converging textual traditions than as a varying reproduction of one archetype[40]. This fact now prevents us from thinking of one recension as the source for the text that is found in the majority of the manuscripts. No matter how one judges about the value of the growing consensus in the textual tradition, one can not simply reduce the large majority of manuscripts to one vote and then only a secondary vote. To say it differently and more technically: it is impossible to treat the majority of the manuscripts during the evaluation of them as though they textually formed one *family*[41]. We do not deny that small family groups can be

1912, p. 51). Against Bardy (op. cit. pp. 178-179) and Metzger (op. cit. p. 6) it can be pointed out that this passage in the *Decr. Gelas.* may be dependent on Hiëronymus' *Praefatio in Evangelio*, but can not be explained from a misunderstanding of his text (cf. note 36). The possibility that the author of the *Decr. Gelas.* also personally knew facts that confirmed what Hiëronymus suggested, is not out of question, because he formulates independently when he specially points to the work of Lucian and Hesychius in the field of the "evangelia".

[39] H. von Soden, *Die Schriften des Neuen Testaments in ihrer ältesten erreichbaren Textgestalt hergestellt auf Grund ihrer Textgeschichte.* I, 2. Göttingen ²1911, pp. 707-893.

[40] K. Lake, The Ecclesiastical Text. (Excursus I to K. Lake, R.P. Blake and S. New, The Caesarean Text of the Gospel of Mark, in: *Harvard Theological Review* 21 [1928] pp. 207-404, esp. pp. 338-357). E.C. Colwell, The complex character of the late byzantine Text of the Gospels (*Journal of Biblical Literature* 54 [1935] pp. 211-221). Compare G. Zuntz, The Byzantine Text in New Testament Criticism (*Journal of Theological Studies* 43 [1942] pp. 25-30). It is striking that a comparable development in the study of the Caesarean text is beginning to show up. See B.M. Metzger, The Caesarean Text of the Gospels (*Chapters in the History of New Testament Textual Criticism* [New Testament Tools and Studies IV]. Leiden 1963, pp. 42-72).

[41] E.C. Colwell defines the term "Family" with the words: ". . . that group of sources whose genealogy can be clearly established so that its text may be reconstructed solely with reference to the external evidence of documents.". *Studies in Methodology in Textual Criticism of the New Testament.* (New Testament Tools and Studies IX). Leiden 1969, p. 11.

distinguished within this majority, just as families can also be determined in other text-types and with the versions. Yet even if the numbers of the different family groups are deducted from the majority of manuscripts, then the Byzantine text still keeps an important majority.

That no importance is attached to this majority as such in modern textual criticism is not only connected with the recension-idea, but especially with the opinion one has concerning the age and character of the Byzantine type. In the reasoning of Hort the arguments regarding age and character also had priority. Only later did Hort begin to think of a recension, possibly by Lucianus. Therefore, in the position of those who reject the Byzantine text, few problems seem to arise if the idea of a recension eventually has to be given up. Whether there was a recension or not, the traditional text still remains just as inferior. Before we deal with these primary arguments in more detail, we must, however, note that the abandonment of the recension-idea does weaken the modern view on the old Church-text. For if it is indeed true that this text has a secondary character, how then can it be accounted for historically that this secondary text received general approval? Hort had an answer to this question at hand: one man made a defective recension due to wrong methods and the Church followed this in good faith. But if this one man (e.g. Lucianus) falls away and also that one recension (e.g. in the 4th century), how can we explain the fact that the tradition is influenced in a negative sense and that this influence promoted *convergence* and *uniformity*. When a text is exposed to gradual deterioration through faults in transmission, it always leads to divergency between various forms of text-corruption and to plurality in the types of degeneration. But history faces us with a tradition which has a convergent character. How can this be accounted for, if the tradition is thought to have deviated from the original and there is no clear revisor's hand in the picture after all? This difficult question can be answered historically, as long as the tradition of the text is not described as secondary. The different centres of production in the 4th and following centuries aimed at a most faithful copy of the original or at a good restoration of the original text. Therefore, after the first centuries of persecution and dearth, a number of traditions automatically appeared which went back to the good text and came close to each other because they all orientated themselves on the most faithful copy of the original. The similar motive explains the trend towards an identical text. Yet how is one to explain that various centres of production, independent of each other, show the same deviations? To say that government intervention caused this similarity in deviation has no historical grounds[42]. If you wish

[42] Growing agreement regarding the text to be followed can not be explained from the interference of the government. This is shown by the fact that still in the 9th century a somewhat deviating text-type is sometimes followed *in Constantinople*. Cf. J.N. Birdsall, The Text of the Gospels in Photius (*Journal of Theological Studies* n.s. 7 [1956] pp. 42-55, 190-198).

the uniforming influence of the liturgy to explain this, then you are only transferring the problem into a different field.

Summarizing we can say that the large number of manuscripts wherein the traditional or Church text occurs, must carry weight. This striking number can not be disqualified with an appeal to Hieronymus' statements about Lucianus of Antioch. It also can not be put aside as meaningless, as though it is to be traced back to one archetype in the 4th century. On the contrary, the large number deserves attention, since, in the midst of all sorts of variation, it confronts us with a growing uniformity. This can hardly be described historically as spontaneous converging deviation. It rather points in the direction of a simultaneous turning-back in various centres to the same central point of the original text. This text was sought in the oldest and most faithful manuscripts, and people conformed to it after centuries of textual disintegration.

The Age of the Byzantine Type

One of the first things a student must learn regarding the textual history, is the distinction between the age of the *manuscript* and the age of the *text* offered in that manuscript. A rather young manuscript can give a very old type of text. This is a true and interesting proposition. You would expect that this proposition would have the result, that people in the modern New Testament textual criticism would hardly argue from the age of the manuscript. However, the opposite is the case. Time and again you come across a comparison between "older manuscripts" and "many, but younger manuscripts". The common argument used against the Byzantine text-type is even that this type is only found in young manuscripts. This argument, however, does not say anything as such. One must prove that the *text-form* in these manuscripts is also of later date.

Hort tried to prove this with an appeal to the fact that the Church Fathers before Nicea did not use a Byzantine text. Now he himself admits that one must be cautious when dealing with the New Testament quotations in the writings of the Church Fathers[43]. In the progress of the textual tradition these quotations have often been altered to fit later text-types. It also often appears that the Church Fathers only quoted in part and freely, so that one can hardly conclude from the form of their quotation the form of the text they read in the New Testament. The value of Hort's arguments is limited even more drastically when he has to admit that we only have clear patristic material from the period 175-250 A.D.[44]. It surely did not escape Hort that two of the Greek Fathers in this period mentioned by him (Irenaeus and Hippolytus) lived in the West. The other two (Clement of Alexandria and Origen) come from Egypt. This means that we are left with a blank spot on the map: What would the text of Church Fathers from Antioch have looked like in this period? We do not know. That we encounter text-usage which is not clearly Byzantine in the writings that have been preserved for us[45] is not surprising. These Church writers used the texts that were current. The form of their text is not necessarily better than that of the manuscripts circulating in their region. But then the pressing question is whether they lived at a time and in a region in which the textual tradition was at its best, or in a time and region in which this tradition was just disturbed by all sorts of influences in the 2nd

[43] Hort, *Introduction* pp. 110-112.

[44] Hort, *Introduction* p. 112.

[45] Here we will not touch upon the question, to what extent the text of these Church Fathers can be brought up against a certain text-*type* (the Byzantine) on the ground of *incidental* variant readings.

century. Hort considers Origen to be the most impressive witness[46], because this scholar is thought to have been acquainted with all the text-types that were in circulation. Metzger, however, showed by means of an examination of Origen's explicit statements on New Testament textual matters that this scholar should certainly not be considered representative of the number of readings current at his time, and that he was also terribly self-willed in his treatment of the textual material[47]. This makes it even more doubtful whether it is possible to prove much from quotations in the writings of Church Fathers in this period.

How cautiously one must, in general, treat proof for textual matters derived from the Church Fathers has been shown quite recently by Prigent[48] and Frede[49] concerning the Greek and Latin Fathers. How the data can often be interpreted in various ways is also shown by the fact that Boismard even develops the hypothesis that a separate Church Father text-type can be distinguished[50]. It is often difficult to evaluate the facts. Mees showed this with regard to the quotations in the writings of Clement of Alexandria[51]. After a thorough study on the Gospel according to John in the writings of Aphrahat (beginning 4th century) Baarda gives a provisional conclusion on the text-type that Aphrahat followed and points out that his text stands nearest to the Egyptian text[52]. Yet on the basis of the data given by Baarda one could claim with even more right that Aphrahat's text stands nearest to the Byzantine type[53]. This last example at the same time illustrates the difficulty that remains if one con-

[46] Hort, *Introduction* p. 114.

[47] B.M. Metzger, Explicit References in the Works of Origen to Variant Readings in New Testament Manuscripts (J.N. Birdsall, R.W. Thomson [eds.], *Biblical and Patristic Studies in Memory of R.P. Casey*. Freiburg 1963, pp. 78-95).

[48] P. Prigent, Les citations des Pères Grecs et la critique textuelle du Nouveau Testament (K. Aland [ed.], *Die alten Ubersetzungen des Neuen Testaments, die Kirchenväterzitate und Lektionare*. [Arbeiten zur neutestamentlichen Textforschung]. Berlin 1972, pp. 436-454).

[49] H.J. Frede, Die Zitate des Neuen Testaments bei den lateinischen Kirchenvätern (K. Aland [ed.], *Die alten Übersetzungen* pp. 455-478).

[50] Review and analysis of Boismard's studies on the text of John can be found in the article of B.M. Metzger, Patristic Evidence and the Textual Criticism of the New Testament (*New Testament Studies* 18 [1971-2] pp. 379-400). M.J. Suggs agrees with Boismard in, Eusebius' Text of John in the "Writings against Marcellus" (*Journal of Biblical Literature* 75 [1956] pp. 137-142).

[51] M. Mees, *Die Zitate aus dem Neuen Testament bei Clemens von Alexandrien*. (Quaderni di "Vetera Christianorum" 2) Bari 1970, I pp. 187-188.

[52] T. Baarda, *The Gospel Quotations of Aphrahat the Persian Sage. I. Aphrahat's Text of the Fourth Gospel*. Thesis Amsterdam 1975, p. 363.

[53] A relevant variation between the Egyptian and the Byzantine text occurs only in 7 instances in the passages from the Gospel according to John discussed by Baarda. In one of these cases the text of Aphrahat can only be established by reconstruction (1:18b); in 3 cases the text of Aphrahat can be regarded as condensed quotation (1:51, 3:34b-35; 13:6) and in 1 case as an expanded quotation (6:52). The two passages in which a comparison is certainly possible (3:13; 5:25) both do *not* offer the Egyptian text, but the Byzantine text.

cludes that the Byzantine text was unknown before Nicea on the basis of a few Church Fathers from a limited number of regions. How can this text then directly afterwards suddenly be known, for example, in the writings of Eustathius of Antioch (beginning 4th century)[54], and in the writings of the Syrian Aphrahat? How can this text then be found in a section of Chrysostom's works[55] as the known text? One could say: this now proves that this Byzantine text was made at the time of Nicea. But how did it manage to spread so quickly? Through what influence? And why are there no indications, in the writings of the 4th century, that the writers were aware that they were introducing a newer text?

From a historical point of view, a different reconstruction of the facts is more plausible. The fact that the Byzantine text is already used in the 4th century as a normal text proves that it must be from an earlier date and was not regarded as "new". If this text is not distinctly followed by Egyptian Fathers and at the same time is found in the first surviving writings from Antioch and its surroundings, then we have every reason to suppose that our view on the most ancient textual history would change considerably if we knew more about the blank spot that is left over on the historical map: Antioch before the 4th century. This is not even so strange. Antioch was the first church to send out missionaries to the heathen and was the base from which Paul and Barnabas worked. As such it is one of the first churches concerning which we may assume that it possessed old archives with early copies of Gospels and Letters. Our unfamiliarity with this section of church history does not give us the right to limit the textual history of the first three centuries to what the scarce remaining data portray to us. A person who has insufficient data for making a reconstruction of an old building, is still not permitted to assume that the original building looked like the ruins that he is left with.

Also without the reasoning from patristic quotations many still consider it to be an established fact that the Byzantine text-form is a *younger* text. The fact that this text-form is known to us via later manuscripts is as such no proof for a late text-type, but it does seem to become a proof when at the same time a different text is found in all older manuscripts. The combination of these two things seems to offer decisive proof for the late origin of the traditional text. How would you otherwise be able to explain that exactly the older known majuscules do *not* offer the Byzantine text and that this text is found in younger majuscules and minus-

[54] M. Spanneut, La Bible d'Eusthate d'Antioche — Contribution à l'histoire de la "version lucianique" (F.L. Cross [ed.], *Studia Patristica* IV, II [Texte und Untersuchungen 79]. Berlin 1961, pp. 171-190).

[55] C.D. Dicks, The Matthean Text of Chrysostom in his Homilies on Matthew (*Journal of Biblical Literature* 67 [1948] pp. 365-376), points, on the one hand, to differences that can be pointed out between the text of Chrysostom and the Koine-text, but suggests, on the other hand, that Chrysostom and not Lucian was the "originator of the K text-type" (p. 376). Here Dicks, however, neglects the fact that Chrysostom in no way shows that he acts as renewer of the text, but constantly claims to follow the well-known text.

cules? Here the material seems convincing. And it is difficult to hold the attention when one wishes to challenge this. If you do not yield to the facts in this matter, then you receive the image of an obscurantist. Even before the contra-arguments are mentioned, there is a certain amount of boredom among the listeners.

Let us therefore reverse the matter. Let us make ourselves aware of *what* we have presupposed with this seemingly convincing argumentation. What conditions must be satisfied if we wish to award the prize to the older majuscules? While asking this question we assumed wittingly or unwittingly that we were capable of making a fair comparison between manuscripts in an earlier period and those in a later period. After all, we can only arrive at positive statements if that is the case. Imagine that someone said: in the Middle Ages mainly cathedrals were built, but in modern times many small and plainer churches are being built. This statement seems completely true when we today look around in the cities and villages. Yet we are mistaken. An understandable mistake: many small churches of the Middle Ages have disappeared, and usually only the cathedrals were restored. Thus, a great historical falsification of perspective with regard to the history of church-building arises. We are not able to make a general assertion about church-building in the Middle Ages on the basis of the surviving materials. If we would still dare to make such an assertion, then we wrongly assumed that the surviving materials enabled us to make a fair comparison. But how is the situation in the field of New Testament manuscripts? Do we have a *representative* number of manuscripts from the first centuries? Only if that is the case, do we have the right to make conclusions and positive statements. Yet it is just at this point that difficulties arise. The situation is even such that we know with certainty that we *do not* possess a representative number of manuscripts from the first centuries. This is due to three reasons, which now deserve our attention successively.

1. From the 2nd and 3rd centuries we only have papyri at our disposal. Due to climatic conditions these can practically only come to us from Egypt. For this period we, therefore, only possess representatives of Egyptian editions of the New Testament. Here we should bear in mind that Egypt was not the most flourishing part of the Church at that time. Centres like Syria, Asia-Minor, Greece, Italy have left us no Greek manuscripts from these centuries. Furthermore, regarding the papyri we should bear in mind that they are not representative library-copies from Alexandria, but cheaper editions circulating in Egypt. A number of them were rediscovered more or less accidently. These finds are very important: also the scarce data have scientific value. But the fact that the finds are incidental and restricted to certain areas, prevents us from generalizing about *the* New Testament text in the first centuries on the ground of this

material. It is not even possible to generalize about *the* Egyptian text of those days on the basis of this material[56].

2. In the codicology the great value of the transliteration-process in the 9th century and thereafter is recognized[57]. At that time the most important New Testament manuscripts written in majuscule script were carefully transcribed into minuscule script. It is assumed that after this transliteration-process the majuscule was taken out of circulation[58]. This is also the conclusion of Lake: copyists destroyed their original after it had been "renewed"[59]. The import of this datum has not been taken into account enough in the present New Testament textual criticism. For it implies, that just the oldest, best and most customary manuscripts come to us in the new uniform of the minuscule script, does it not? This is even more cogent, since it appears that various archetypes can be detected in this transliteration-process for the New Testament. Therefore we do not receive one mother-manuscript through the flood-gates of the transliteration, but several[60]. The originals have, however, disappeared! This throws a totally different light on the situation that we are confronted with regarding the manuscripts. Why do the surviving ancient manuscripts show another text-type? Because they are the only survivors of their generation, and because their survival is due to the fact that they were of a different kind. Even though one continues to maintain that the copyists at the time of the transliteration handed down the wrong text-type to the Middle Ages, one can still never prove this codicologically with the remark that older majuscules have a different text. This would be circular reasoning. There certainly were majuscules just as venerable and ancient as the surviving Vaticanus or Sinaiticus, which, like a section of the Alexandrinus, presented a Byzantine text. But they have been renewed into minuscule script and their majuscule-appearance has vanished. His-

[56] A.F.J. Klijn even concludes on the basis of the papyri the existence of *two* text-types circulating in Egypt: *A Survey of the Researches into the Western Text of the Gospels and Acts.* II (1949-1969). (Supplements to Novum Testamentum 21). Leiden 1969, pp. 48-50. R. Kieffer considers the one type as a recension of the other type: *Au delà des recensions? L'Evolution de la tradition textuelle dans Jean VI, 52-71.* (Coniectanea Biblica. NT Series 3). Lund 1968, pp. 244-245.

[57] A. Dain, *Les manuscrits*. Paris 1949, pp. 111-120.

[58] A. Dain, *Les manuscrits*. Paris 1949, p. 115: "L'exemplaire translitteré, soigneusement écrit et solidement relié, devenait le point de départ de la tradition ultérieure. Les vieux modèles de papyrus ou de parchemin, sans doute très usés, qui avaient servi à sa confection n'offraient plus aucun intérêt. Ils étaient normalement abandonnés ou détruits.".

[59] "Taking this fact into consideration along with the negative result of our collation of MSS. at Sinai, Patmos and Jerusalem, it is hard to resist the conclusion, that the scribes usually destroyed their exemplars when they had copied the sacred books.": K. Lake, The Ecclesiastical Text pp. 348-349 (complete title in note 40).

[60] The minuscule-tradition of the New Testament text can not be brought down to one archetype (cf. the literature mentioned in note 40). Compare also J.N. Birdsall, The New Testament Text (P.R. Ackroyd, C.F. Evans [eds.], *The Cambridge History of the Bible. Volume I: From the Beginnings to Jerome.* Cambridge 1970, pp. 308-377, esp. 314-316).

torically it *seems* as though the most ancient majuscule manuscripts exclusively contain a non-Byzantine text, but the prespective is falsified here just like it is regarding church-building in the Middle Ages and at present.

3. That the older majuscule text is not representative of *the* ancient text of the New Testament has been shown even more clearly in the 20th century than was possible in Hort's days. The papyri which have been found and published in the meantime have, namely, made it clear that it is not possible anymore to consider with Hort the codex Vaticanus purely as a restored "Neutral" text[61]. In the Vaticanus we find one of the text-types that were current in Egypt. And this is certainly not the original text just like that. Moreover, the papyri have shown clearly that readings which do not occur in the older majuscules and therefore were called late and Byzantine, do occur in the 2nd and 3rd century: although they did not have a place in the older majuscules, they do have a place in the still older papyri[62]! Rightly so, we have been warned not to over-estimate the cogency of this fact: it is not true that the papyri offer a Byzantine text[63]. But here we must also warn against under-estimating this datum: Zuntz and others conclude from it, at the least, that readings which look like Byzantine, can be old[64]. However, this conclusion essentially makes the rejection of the Byzantine text uncertain. For, going further back into the

[61] K. Aland, Die Bedeutung des P[75] für den Text des Neuen Testaments. Ein Beitrag zur Frage der "Western non-interpolations" (K. Aland, *Studien zur Überlieferung des Neuen Testaments und seines Textes*. [Arbeiten zur neutestamentlichen Textforschung II]. Berlin 1967, pp. 155-172).

[62] G. Zuntz, *The Text of the Epistles. A Disquisition upon the Corpus Paulinum.* London 1953, p. 55: "To sum up. A number of Byzantine readings, most of them genuine, which previously were discarded as "late", are anticipated by P[46]. Our inquiry has confirmed what was anyhow probable enough: the Byzantines did not hit upon these readings by conjecture or independent error. They reproduced an older tradition.". It is remarkable how these facts are sometimes annexed by the New Testament textual criticism. In the 20th century people have, on the ground of overestimation of some manuscripts, omitted certain passages from Luke 24, which occur in nearly all the manuscripts. Now that these passages also appear to occur in an ancient papyrus, they are again admitted in the text. But now the "ancient" and unjustly abandoned text is presented as the newest result of modern scholarship. H. Kunst writes: "Hier sehen wir die Fortschritte der modernen Textkritik im Vergleich zu der vergangener Generationen einmal in hellem Licht: einer der berühmten Bodmer-Papyri (P[75] aus dem Anfang des 3. Jahrhunderts, 1961 zum erstenmal veröffentlicht) lieferte die Voraussetzung für diese Entscheidungen, die nun für alle wissenschaftliche Exegese wie alle praktische Auslegung von grundlegender Bedeutung sind.". Here the credit for the ancient text is ascribed to oneself by a scholarship which had wrongly abandoned this text! (*Bericht der Stiftung zur Förderung der neutestamentlichen Textforschung für die Jahre 1972 bis 1974*. Münster 1974, p. 35).

[63] B.M. Metzger, *Chapters in the History of New Testament Textual Criticism*. (New Testament Tools and Studies IV). Leiden 1963, pp. 38-39. E.C. Colwell, *Studies in Methodology in Textual Criticism of the New Testament*. (New Testament Tools and Studies IX). Leiden 1969, p. 52.

[64] G. Zuntz, *The Text of the Epistles. A Disquisition upon the Corpus Paulinum.* London 1953, pp. 56; 150-151; 283.

past has now shown — and that in Egyptian documents — that a number of "late" readings really are "old". What reason do we still have to state that other Byzantine readings are not old: it has now been proven that what we today consider "young" can tomorrow be shown to be "old". And this has been proven while we were only able to look into one incidental fragment of the text from the first centuries. According to the theory of Hort the number of "Byzantine" readings would become less the further we go back into the past. Yet it seems to be increasing! This gives us the liberty to assume for the present that still more "young" readings would be able to prove their identity if we had more and older material at our disposal. We do not derive this liberty from the occurrence of these "Byzantine" readings in the papyri as such. We derive it from the surprising circumstance that in an unexpected area (Egypt!) the "Byzantine" readings do not decrease, but increase, the deeper we penetrate into the first centuries. If the modern scholarship of the New Testament textual criticism did not have that prejudice against the Byzantine text, then there would be every reason to hypothesize a gradual "de-byzantinizing" of the text, which resulted in the text-type of the older surviving majuscules, and which was reversed in the remainder of the textual tradition. A complete proof for this hypothesis can not be given. Yet the present state of the data does make it more plausible to follow this hypothesis than to maintain that the Byzantine text is from a later date, while at the same time one must reluctantly add to the list of "ancient Byzantine readings".

To conclude these three arguments supporting the view that the number of surviving manuscripts is not representative of the first centuries, we still wish to point to an analogue elsewhere. Streeter, who considers the recension of Lucianus in *the 4th century* as historical, writes that this recension is found for the first time in a pure form in manuscripts from *the 9th century*.

> "It may at first sight seem surprising that, alike on von Soden's and on Mrs. Lake's view, the purest form of the text of Lucian's recension should be preserved in MSS not earlier than the ninth century . . . . The fact, however, becomes easily explicable when we remember that in the ninth century there was a notable revival of learning in the Byzantine Empire. A natural result of this would be to cause Christian scholars to seek a better text of the Gospels by going back from current texts to more ancient MSS . . . . An analogy may be found in the effect of the revival of learning under Charlemagne on the text of the Latin classics. MSS of the seventh and eighth centuries — I derived the information from the late Prof. A.C. Clark — are full of corruptions which do not occur in MSS of the subsequent period"[65].

For now we leave undecided whether Streeter's view concerning a Lucian recension is correct or not. We wish to point out how *legitimate* he considers the thought that later manuscripts, despite their youth, offer the most ancient text. Why may not this thought also be advanced con-

[65] B.H. Streeter, The early Ancestry of the Textus Receptus of the Gospels (*Journal of Theological Studies* 38 [1937] pp. 225-229, esp. p. 229).

cerning the Byzantine text as such, when the limited character of the material and the circumstances of papyri-finds and transliteration give every reason for it? In addition, it is historically certain that the text of the New Testament endured a very hard time in the first centuries. Many good and official editions of the text were confiscated and destroyed by the authorities during the time of the persecutions[66]. Moreover, the heretics in the 2nd century did not hesitate to alter the text and thereby bring the textual tradition in confusion[67]. Thirdly, copyists and philologists did not always understand their responsibility properly: in the first centuries there was a great deal of text-revision whereby eventually the contact with the original threatened to disappear[68]. Only after the third century the Church received the opportunity to put things in order also regarding the text. These are known facts from history. They support the view that manuscripts from the first centuries do not always offer a better and more ancient text than the manuscripts from later centuries.

Summarizing we must conclude that the codicology and the history of text-corruption and text-preservation plead in favour of the antiquity of the so-called Byzantine text-type; that the absence of this type in the more ancient majuscules and in the writings of some Egyptian Church Fathers before Nicea can not be used as argument against this antiquity.

[66] Eusebius, *Historia Ecclesiastica* VIII, II, I. 4. Cf. F.H.A. Scrivener, *A Plain Introduction to the Criticism of the New Testament*. Fourth Edition edited by E. Miller. II. London 1894, pp. 265-266.

[67] See E. Nestle, *Einführung in das Griechische Neue Testament.* Göttingen ³1909, pp. 219-232.

[68] Hiëronymus, *Epistula LXXI,* 5. B.M. Metzger, *The Text of the New Testament. Its Transmission, Corruption and Restoration*. Oxford ²1968, pp. 152; 195-196. G. Zuntz, *The Text of the Epistles. A Disquisition upon the Corpus Paulinum*. London 1953, p. 262. For "Alexandrian textual criticism", compare W.R. Farmer, *The Last Twelve Verses of Mark*. (SNTS Mon. Series 25). Cambridge 1974, pp. 13-22.

The Nature of the Byzantine Type

For many people the real and decisive argument against the antiquity of the Byzantine text-type lies in the *nature* and *character* of this text. It is thought to be evident from the type itself that we have a *secondary* type here before us. Hort speaks of an internal evidence. If you analyse the seemingly external evidence of Hort, you discover that indeed his whole genealogical system can be traced back to an evaluation of readings on internal grounds[69]. Thus his rejection of the so-called Syrian text is ultimately based on internal evidence, on the kind of reading and the kind of text found in it. And when Metzger in his Textual Commentary almost a century later typifies the Byzantine text according to its nature, he also begins with pointing out the evident secondary character of this text-form. Herein he follows Hort completely. The latter wrote:

> "The qualities which the authors of the Syrian text seem to have most desired to impress on it are lucidity and completeness. They were evidently anxious to remove all stumbling-blocks out of the way of the ordinary reader . . . ."[70]

Metzger writes:

> "It (The Byzantine Text) is characterized chiefly by lucidity and completeness. The framers of this text sought to smooth away any harshness of language, to combine two or more divergent readings into one expanded reading (called conflation), and to harmonize divergent parallel passages."[71]

This judgement concerning the Byzantine type is accepted today by many upon authority of these and other writers. Yet this judgement has not been proven, and can not be proven. Often illustrative examples are given to support this negative characterization of the Byzantine text. But it would not be difficult to "prove", with the aid of specially chosen examples from other text-types, that those types are also guilty of harmonizing, conflating readings and smoothing the diction[72]. Here illustrations do not prove anything. After all, one could without much difficulty give a

[69] Hort, *Introduction* pp. 40-41, writes that the *readings* can be reduced to their one origin with the aid of the genealogy of the *manuscripts*. However, later on, Hort, *Introduction* p. 46, admits that a genealogy of the *manuscripts* can not very well be determined on external, bibliographical grounds. He then reconstructs the genealogy on the ground of the *readings*. Here Hort is, however, moving from the origin of the manuscripts to the origin of the readings, while accepting that "identity of reading implies identity of origin". The latter is, however, a debatable axiom and is certainly insufficient to base a genealogy on it. G.D. Fee agrees with Hort on the point of the evaluation of manuscripts on the basis of the readings (non-genealogical): P^{75}, P^{66}, and Origen: The Myth of early textual Recension in Alexandria (in: R.N. Longenecker, M.C. Tenney [eds.], *New Dimensions in New Testament Study*. Grand Rapids 1974, pp. 19-45).

[70] Hort, *Introduction* p. 134.

[71] B.M. Metzger, *A Textual Commentary on the Greek New Testament*. London 1971, p. xx.

[72] Cf. E.F. Hills, Harmonizations in the Caesarean Text of Mark (*Journal of Biblical Literature* 66 [1947] pp. 135-152).

large number of examples from the Byzantine text to support the proposition that this text does *not* harmonize and does *not* smooth away. In commentaries the exegete is often satisfied with the incidental example without comparing it to the textual data as a whole. Yet a proposition about the Byzantine *type* should not be based on illustrations, but on arguments from the text *as a whole*. Whoever wishes to find such arguments, will meet a number of methodical problems and obstacles, which obstruct the way to the proof. Here we can mention the following points:

1. Methodically we must first ask how a "type" is determined. This can not be done on the basis of selected readings, because then the selection will soon be determined by what one is trying to prove. You can only speak of a text-type if the characteristics which must distinguish the type are not incidental but are found all along, and if they do not appear in other types from which the type must be distinguished[73]. The criteria must be distinctive and general. As far as this is concerned, suspicion is roused when Hort remarks that the harmonizing and assimilating interpolations in the Byzantine text are "fortunately capricious and incomplete"[74]. Did Hort then indeed generalize and make characteristics of some readings into characteristics of the text-type? This suspicion becomes certainty when Metzger in his *Textual Commentary* has to observe more than once that non-Byzantine readings, for example, in the codex Vaticanus, can be explained from the tendencies of scribes to assimilate and to simplify the text[75]. What is typical for the Byzantine text is apparently not so exclusive for this text-type! But if certain phenomena seem to appear in all types of text, then it is not right to condemn a type categorically and regard it as secondary on the ground of such phenomena.

[73] E.C. Colwell, *Studies in Methodology in Textual Criticism of the New Testament*. (New Testament Tools and Studies IX). Leiden 1969, pp. 10-11: "The members of the group must share some readings that do not appear outside the group.". "The second objective criterion for the existence of a Text-type is the agreement of a group of manuscripts in a large majority of the total readings where the manuscript evidence is divided.".

[74] Hort, *Introduction* p. 135.

[75] We offer a small number of examples chosen at random from various sections of Metzger's *Textual Commentary*. Matthew 19:3 ("On the other hand, in view of the predominantly Alexandrian character of the evidence supporting the shorter text, the Committee judged that it is somewhat more probable that the word was deleted in the interest of producing a more concise literary style."). Matthew 19:9 ("It is probable that the witnesses . . . which have the former reading have been assimilated to 5:32, where the text is firm."). John 6:14 (". . . the plural seems to be the result of scribal assimilation to 2:23 and 6:2."). James 2:3 ("Not recognizing this, B and several other witnesses . . . transposed *ekei* so as to produce a parallellism of two (rather than three) references to places."). James 4:14 (". . . in view of a certain tendency of B to omit the article . . ."). James 5:16 (". . . the result of scribal conformation to the customary Christian usage."). James 5:20 (". . . appears to be an amelioration, having been introduced either in order to conform to the address . . ., or in order to avoid the ambiguity of who is to be regarded (the converter or the converted) as the subject of the verb."). *The quoted negative statements are all related to readings in the Codex Vaticanus and not to the Byzantine text.*

2. Moreover, it is methodically difficult to speak of harmonizing and assimilating deviations in a text, when the original is not known. Or is it an axiom that the original text in any case was so inharmonious, that every harmonious reading is directly suspect? Hort lets us sense that he personally does not prefer a New Testament "more fitted for cursory perusal or recitation than for repeated and diligent study"[76]. Yet who, without the original at his disposal, can prove that this original had those characteristics which a philologist and a textual critic considers to be most recommendable?

3. Although Hort worked a lot on the arguments from conflation, it appears that only a very limited number of readings can be found in the Byzantine text to serve as examples of conflation[77]. The so-called phenomenon of conflation is also not typically Byzantine; one can also point to it in the codex Vaticanus, for example[78]. It is for that matter still the question whether that which is called "conflation" rightly deserves that name. When two possible readings are clearly placed beside each other in a text as alternative readings, one can speak of conflation. But that hardly ever occurs. A "conflate reading" as a rule applies to longer readings which offer a flowing text and which can only be called a conflate reading because two types of shorter readings are known to occur in other manuscripts and are considered to be the materials for the compound and longer reading. Kilpatrick has shown, however, that many of these shorter readings can equally well be described as reduction-readings with regard to the longer and original reading[79].

4. If editors of the Byzantine text would have been out to harmonize the text and to fit parallel passages of the Gospels into each other, then

[76] Hort, *Introduction* p. 135. P. Walters, *The Text of the Septuagint. Its Corruptions and their Emendation*. Edited by D.W. Gooding. Cambridge 1973, p. 21, writes: "Hort's sense of style, his idea of what was correct and preferable in every alternative, was acquired from a close acquaintance with his "neutral" text. It did not occur to him that most of its formal aspects tallied with his standards just because these were taken from his model. So far his decisions are in the nature of a vicious circle. We today who live outside this magic circle, which kept a generation spellbound, are able to see through Hort's illusion. In fact we know that the traits which were congenial to Hort's mind, the abstention from extremes, or at least well-tempered moderation in admitting them, are the unmistakable mark of *recension*.".

[77] Hort only discussed 8 examples as basis for his theory that the *whole* Byzantine text-tradition, also because of its conflate character, must be abandoned. These 8 examples are only derived from Mark (4) and Luke (4).

[78] B.M. Metzger, *Textual Commentary* writes in Colossians 1:12, after he has discussed two variant readings: "The reading of B is an early conflation of both variants.". Seeing only B has this longer reading, the probability that we have a conflate reading here is far greater than in the 8 cases discussed by Hort, because the so-called conflate readings of the Byzantine text do not only occur in this text-tradition, but also elsewhere, in other traditions or old translations.

[79] G.D. Kilpatrick, The Greek New Testament Text of Today and the Textus Receptus (H. Anderson, W. Barclay [eds.], *The New Testament in Historical and Contemporary Perspective. Essays in Memory of G.H.C. Macgregor*. Oxford 1965, pp. 189-208, esp. 190-193).

we must observe that they let nearly all their opportunities go by. When one follows the Byzantine text, all problems with apparent contradictions in the Gospels are just as strongly present as in modern text editions, and that while the Church in the fourth century was also confronted with the criticism on the Gospels from the Neoplatonic school[80]. Yet there is no question of an "easier" text in the Gospels with the Byzantine text-type. The Church did defend the harmony of the Gospels during the time of Augustine, but did not, at will, force it upon the text by means of harmonizing redaction[81]. In addition, what seems to be harmonization is in a different direction often no harmonization. A reading may seem adjusted to the parallel passage in an other Gospel, but then often deviates again from the reading in the third Gospel. A reading may seem borrowed from the parallel story, yet at the same time fall out of tune in the context of the Gospel itself. Here the examples are innumerable as long as one does not limit himself to a few texts and pays attention to the context and the Gospels as a whole[82]. We confine ourselves to one small illustration. In Mark 10:47 Nestle gives the reading *Nazarènos* and not the reading that among others occurs in the Byzantine text: *Nazooraios*. In the critical apparatus the last-mentioned reading is accounted for as an assimilation to the parallel place Luke 18:37 where *Nazooraios* is found. One

[80] H. Merkel, *Die Widersprüche zwischen den Evangelien. Ihre polemische und apologetische Behandlung in der Alten Kirche bis zu Augustin*. (Wissenschaftl. Untersuchungen zum Neuen Testament 13). Tübingen 1971, pp. 13-23; 218-261.

[81] Harmonizing redaction, with the aid of the Gospel according to Matthew as norm, is pointed out regarding the Alexandrian philologists in the 3rd century by W.R. Farmer. He considers it possible that this explains the omission of Mark 16:9-20 from a *limited* section of the manuscripts: " 'Faithful' and 'circumspect' teachers like Origen generally speaking would not have argued for the omission of a textual reading that had been received in the church. But insofar as they were trained in the ways of Alexandrian text criticism *and had a concern for what was edifying for the church* they would have tended to respect received exemplars which omitted this kind of doubtful reading, and in some situations could have tolerated and perhaps even approved the production and use of copies of Mark ending with ἐφοβοῦντο γάρ. This would help explain the fact that the Cappadocian Fathers, all of whom were of the Alexandrian school, make no reference to Mark 16:9-20. And further, because of the influence of the Cappadocians on the Armenian church, it would help explain why the Armenian version omitted these verses. In this way a theory of textual development can be posited which accounts for most of the evidence bearing on the question of the external witnesses for and against the authenticity of the last twelve verses of Mark.". *The Last Twelve Verses of Mark*. (SNTS Mon. Series 25). Cambridge 1974, p. 71.

[82] The comparison of the edition Stephanus (1550) with Nestle-Aland (25th edition) led to the result that the dilemma "harmonizing/not harmonizing" is unsuited to distinguish both of these text-editions. We examined Matthew 5:1-12; 6:9-13; 13:1-20; 19:1-12; Mark 2:18-3:6; Luke 9:52-62; 24:1-12; John 6:22-71; Acts 18:18-19:7; 22:6-21; I Corinthians 7; James 3:1-10; 5:10-20; Revelation 5. In the comparative examination not only the context, but also all the parallel passages were taken into account. Since the Stephanus-text is closely related to the Byzantine text and the edition Nestle-Aland is clearly non-Byzantine, the result of this investigation may also apply to the relation between the Byzantine text and other text-types: the dilemma "harmonizing/not harmonizing" or "assimilating/not assimilating" is unsound to distinguish *types* in the textual tradition of the New Testament.

could, however, with just as much right call the reading *Nazarènos* an assimilating reading within Mark: this writer, after all, also uses the form *Nazarènos* the other three times! Did the tradition that reads *Nazarènos* in Mark 10:47 now assimilate to the usage of Mark, or did the tradition that reads *Nazooraios* assimilate to the parallel message in Luke? The questions show that we are trying to force on the textual data a dilemma which does not fit the data[83]. Time and again it appears that the text-phenomena are not adequately treated if we wish to force them into the scheme of readings which harmonize and readings which do not harmonize[84].

5. Metzger mentions as one of the characteristics of the Byzantine text the removing of linguistically difficult expressions and the smoothing out of the text. Kilpatrick, however, has shown that the opposite is true. The Byzantine readings can often be described as a linguistic restoration, after semitic expressions had been eliminated in the second century, poor Greek had been improved, and the text had been made more "Attic" at various points. Kilpatrick concludes: "Our principal conclusion is that the Syrian text is frequently right. It has avoided at many points mistakes and deliberate changes found in other witnesses"[85]. This does not mean that Kilpatrick wishes to canonize every Byzantine reading. Yet his studies do show that one can not speak of a typical secondary character of the Byzantine text as far as the language is concerned[86].

[83] J. van Bruggen, Nazoreeërs, de oudste naam voor christenen (*Almanak Fides Quadrat Intellectum 1973*, Kampen 1973, pp. 147-176).

[84] In Mark 10:34 most manuscripts read "the third day". Metzger, *Textual Commentary* chooses the reading "after three days" and is of the opinion that the original reading "has been conformed by copyists to the much more frequently used expression τῇ τρίτῃ ἡμέρᾳ." Yet in Mark the Byzantine text twice reads "the third day" (9:31; 10:34) and once "after three days" (8:31). In all three places the Egyptian majuscules read "after three days". Therefore one can say with more right, that Mark 9:31 and 10:34 have been *assimilated* to the expression chosen the first time (8:31) by Mark, in these Egyptian manuscripts. The idea that the Byzantine text Mark 10:34 conformed to the usage of Matthew (20:19) and Luke (18:33) is evidently wrong, since such an assimilation in the Byzantine text is just *missing* in Mark 8:31.

[85] Besides the article mentioned in note 79, from which we quoted p. 205, we can mention: Atticism and the Text of the Greek New Testament (J. Blinzler, O. Kuss, F. Mussner [eds.], *Neutestamentliche Aufsätze. Festschrift für J. Schmid*. Regensburg 1963, pp. 125-137); An eclectic Study of the Text of Acts (J.N. Birdsall, R.W. Thomson [eds.], *Biblical and Patristic Studies in Memory of R.P. Casey*. Freiburg 1963, pp. 64-77); Style and Text in the Greek New Testament (B.L. Daniels, M.J. Suggs [eds.], *Studies in the History and Text of the New Testament in Honor of K.W. Clark*. Salt Lake City 1967, pp. 153-160).

[86] C.M. Martini, Eclecticism and Atticism in the Textual Criticism of the Greek New Testament (M. Black, W.A. Smalley [eds.], *On Language, Culture, and Religion: In Honor of E.A. Nida*. The Hague 1974, pp. 149-156), thinks that the establishment of an eclectic text on the basis of the criterion of atticisms encounters the methodical problem of how to determine what must be considered as "atticism" in the 2nd-4th centuries. The objections of Martini against the eclecticism of Kilpatrick, however, also apply to those who wish to abandon the Byzantine text on the basis of the criterion of atticism. Cf. J.K. Elliott, Phrynichus' Influence on the Textual Tradition of the New Testament (*Zeitschrift für die neutestamentliche Wissenschaft* 63 [1972] pp. 133-138).

6. It is difficult to grasp the reproach that the traditional text suffers from its completeness. Maybe it means that as much as possible textual data have been included in this text. The completeness of a text is a good characteristic, is it not? The difficulty only arises when a text offers more than the original. However, one can show that the Byzantine text did *not* include many readings that were in circulation. Mark 16:9-20 can be found in it, but not the so-called comma Johanneum (I John 5:7-8). In Luke 11 one can find a fuller redaction of the Lord's Prayer than in some other manuscripts, but one will not find the words that the Vulgate reads in Acts 9:5b-6a. The passages mentioned do occur in the Greek text, published later, the textus receptus. However one may think about the inclusion of these passages in the textus receptus, one can not ascribe this inclusion to the Byzantine text-tradition. It is true that it has a longer reading than other manuscripts at some points, but it also has at various points a shorter reading than the so-called Western text. The question also applies here: With what is the Byzantine text now being compared? With a personally preferred text, for example, the Vaticanus or the Egyptian text in general? In that case there are certain differences. Yet in the Byzantine text as a whole these differences can not be mentioned as typifying characteristics. They also stand in a different light when we place them in the totality of the circulating traditions, including the Western.

Summarizing we must conclude: the widely spread opinion that the Byzantine text has a secondary character rests on the suggestive force of selected illustrations, but is contrary to the facts as a whole. What is advanced as "typifying" is not distinctive and is not general.

Rehabilitation of the Ancient Text

In the textual criticism of the 20th century, the rejection of the well-known traditional or Byzantine text predominates. That text is even ruled out completely and in advance by the selection-process at Münster. The arguments against this text originate from the 19th century. People are still using them, but without sufficient reason. In fact, much that was raised against this text has crumpled up. The genealogical method is losing ground. Papyri are shown to contain unexpected Byzantine readings. The arguments against this Byzantine text are still less decisive than in the 19th century.

There is, therefore, every reason to rehabilitate the Church text again. It has already been accepted for centuries and centuries by the Greek Church as the ancient and correct text. Its right does not have to be proven. The person who thinks he knows better than those who preserved and transmitted the text in the past should come along with proof. The churches of the great Reformation deliberately adopted this ancient text when they took the Greek text as starting-point again[87]. This text deserves to remain recognized as reliable, unless real contra-proof can be given from a recovered better text. However, there are no better texts. There are theories about a better text and there are reconstructions of such a text, but they can not conceal the fact that, over against the rejection of the ancient, well-known text in the 20th century, only the embarrassment of eclecticism and of a renewed conjectural criticism[88] is left over. Over against this modern textual criticism, we plead for *rehabilitation* of the ancient and well-known text. This means that we do not dismiss this text which is found in a large majority of the textual witnesses and which underlies all the time-honoured Bible translations of the past, but prize and use it[89].

[87] T.H.L. Parker, *Calvin's New Testament Commentaries*. London 1971, pp. 93-123, thinks that Calvin followed the edition Colinaeus in his commentaries between 1540 and 1548, and (probably under influence of Robert Estienne) the text of Erasmus or Stephanus in his later commentaries. Thus Parker sees the young Calvin temporarily as a lonely pioneer heading for a text better than the textus receptus. However, there is no historical indication for the proposition that Calvin chose the edition Colinaeus *as opposed to the other* editions in circulation. Since the edition Colinaeus appeared without Prolegomena, it is even the question whether Calvin was aware of the fact that this edition differed at various points from the other editions at the time. There is nothing to indicate that he consciously made a stand at this point. Even though Calvin does not always use the same edition, his aim has always been to follow the text that the church had followed in previous centuries.

[88] A. Wikenhauser, J. Schmid, *Einleitung in das Neue Testament*. Freiburg [6]1973, pp. 185-186. J. Strugnell, A Plea for conjectural Emendation in the New Testament (*Catholic Biblical Quarterly* 36 [1974] pp. 543-558).

[89] Striking is the plea for the Byzantine text by Ivanov Alexeev in *Zhurnal Moskovskoi Patriarchii* (1954 en 1956), summarized by R.P. Casey in *Theology* 60 (1957) pp. 50-54.

Bringing the well-known, but rejected Byzantine text into use again leads to a totally *different scope of the textual criticism*. It will, in a reformatory sense, set itself the task of preserving this text. Here an appeal can be made to the often unjustly-forgotten work of scholars such as Nolan[90], Reiche[91], Scrivener[92], Burgon[93], Birks[94] and Miller[95], who at the time confronted themselves with the theories of Griesbach, Lachmann and Westcott-Hort. Association with the Byzantine text which was also defended by them implies, in the line of the history, first of all an association with and an emendation of the textus receptus, the printed Greek text from the time of the Reformation. Pleading for the return to the known Church text certainly does not mean that this textus receptus must be canonized. But this pleading does recognize the justice of the principle behind these text-editions of the Reformation. The textus receptus should not be rejected categorically because of its shortcomings, but should according to its own design and intention be corrected conformable to the so-called Byzantine text. This leads to a positively orientated textual criticism, which focuses its attention on all the material handed down, without discrimination.

Association with the text that has been transmitted for such a long time also demands protection of that text. Preservation of manuscripts should be stimulated. The theories of textual criticism, which oppose this text, must also be analysed. Those who wish to hold the well-known text in honour in the 20th century may not overlook the modern text-editions, the product of recent theories. The examination of the modern textual criticism and the readings it defends should, however, not stand in the service of an eclecticism whereby the Byzantine text is only accepted as

[90] F. Nolan, *An Inquiry into the Integrity of the Greek Vulgate or Received Text of the New Testament: in which the Greek Manuscripts are newly classed, the Integrity of the Authorised Text vindicated, and the various readings traced to their origin.* London 1815.

[91] J.G. Reiche, *Commentarius Criticus. III. Epist. ad Hebraeos et Epist. Cathol. continens.* Observatio praevia. Göttingen 1862, pp. 1-6.

[92] F.H.A. Scrivener, *A Plain Introduction to the Criticism of the New Testament*. Fourth Edition edited by E. Miller. I-II. London 1894.

[93] J.W. Burgon, *The Revision Revised*. London 1883. *The Last Twelve Verses of the Gospel according to S. Mark vindicated against recent critical Objectors and established*. Oxford 1871. (Reprint in 1959 with an Introduction by E.F. Hills [Ann Arbor: The Sovereign Grace Book Club]). *The Traditional Text of the Holy Gospels vindicated and established.* Edited by E. Miller. London 1896. *The Causes of Corruption of the Traditional Text of the Holy Gospels*. Edited by E. Miller, London 1896.

[94] T.R. Birks, *Essay on the Right Estimation of Manuscript Evidence in the Text of the New Testament*. London 1878.

[95] E. Miller, *A Guide to the Textual Criticism of the New Testament*. London 1886. *The Present State of the Textual Controversy respecting the Holy Gospels*. (Printed for private circulation) (1898): in this publication Miller gives a retrospect on the *Oxford Debate on the Textual Criticism of the New Testament, held at New College on May 6, 1897 between E. Miller and W. Sanday*, of which the report under this heading was published in London 1897.

one of the sources for optional-readings[96]. Eclecticism is always a subjective matter and only creates new mixed texts. The criteria of eclecticism also contradict each other[97]. Now that considerable agreement concerning the text exists in the broad stream of the text-tradition, there is no need to resort to eclecticism. Copies of a corrupt text-form in the 2nd century, accidentally saved, would then receive a place equal to that of copies from many other centuries which are generally accepted as faithful copies. With this we do not exclude in advance every thought of an emendation of the Byzantine text. But that emendation may only take place if it can be demonstrated clearly to everyone that the Church had lost a good reading or had exchanged it for a bad reading, and why. *In principle* such an argumentation on the ground of external evidence must remain possible, but *in practise* it is almost impossible in the present situation because we only have little and fragmentary textual and historical material from the first centuries. We should guard against wanting to do the work of the fourth and following centuries over again, with less and worse material than people at the time had at their disposal!

The rehabilitation of the received text should, in the churches of the Reformation, result in putting this text into use again, and that first of all for the Bible-*translation*. Translations which go back to the Byzantine text do not need to be old translations[98]. They may even on the mission fields be very new. But the newest translation should still give access to the text of the Church of the ages and not to the text of five learned contemporaries in the 20th century[99]. The *Greek New Testament* of the *United Bible Societies* should as basis for translations of the New Testament be exchanged for an edition of the textus receptus, possibly in an emended form. Also the *exegesis* should turn back to this text. Thus the way to commentaries from many centuries, which all confidently explained this

[96] Thus in F.H.A. Scrivener, *A Plain Introduction to the Criticism of the New Testament*. Fourth Edition edited by E. Miller. II. London 1894, pp. 300-301.

[97] A reading which is preferable because of "the style and vocabulary of the author throughout the book" or because of "the immediate context" is on the other hand often suspect as *lectio facilior*. When one takes into account the possibility that the scribe omits "material which he deemed to be (i) superfluous, (ii) harsh, or (iii) contrary to pious belief, liturgical usage, or ascetical practice" one often comes in conflict with the rule *lectio brevior potior*. Cf. Metzger, *Textual Commentary* pp. xxvi-xxviii. The criterion of the authenticity of the reading which can explain the origin of the other variants can not be applied objectively: when reading B via "transcriptional probability" can be described as derived from reading A, reading A can often via "redactional probability" be described as derived from reading B.

[98] It is deplorable that S. Tregelles, who clearly demanded the recognition of the Holy Scriptures as God's Word for the work of Bible-*translation*, let himself be influenced greatly by the neutralism of his days in the field of the *text*. See H.R. Jones, *Samuel Tregelles 1813-1875. Background to modern Translations of the Bible*. Annual Lecture of the Evangelical Library, London 1975.

[99] Compare at this point also the similar opinion of Bengel, quoted in G. Mälzer, *Johann Albrecht Bengel. Leben und Werk*. Stuttgart 1970, p. 178.

Church text, is again opened. Contact and fellowship with the history of the exegesis is essential for the explanation of Scripture in the 20th century. During a theological training the student must be made acquainted with both the edition of Nestle and the textus receptus. Yet in the exegesis he does not have to give up his faith in the traditional text because of a recent edition, even though it be frequently used. That Church text, and a good edition of it, should form the basis and the material for the exegesis.

This pleading for rehabilitation of the well-known text, however, runs up against the difficulty that a *text-edition* of this text is no longer provided for and that the text of centuries and centuries can often only be obtained second-hand. In this situation it is not permitted to wait for a republication of the textus receptus until it can be offered in a still somewhat improved edition. An edition of the traditional text, as this was printed in the time of the Reformation, must first of all again be obtainable as soon as possible. The return to the Church text also in Bible-translation and exegesis can not be effectuated until such an edition is again available. In connection with this we can mention with thankfulness the initiative which the *Trinitarian Bible Society* has taken to republish the Greek text that was followed in the Authorized Version. For this purpose they associate themselves with an edition of this text that Scrivener at the time took care of[100]. This text deviates from the text of Beza's Greek New Testament only to a low degree and can be described as a variant of the textus receptus or of the Stephanus-edition 1550. Thanks to this edition there is now, over against the edition of the United Bible Societies which purposefully abandons the traditional text, also a Greek text available which deliberately wishes to follow that text.

Perhaps it is possible in the future that a revised new edition of Scrivener's Editio Maior[101] appears besides this text-edition: also the opponents of the Byzantine text will admit that it is desirable for scientific study to possess a text-edition, wherein one can accurately and instantly see where modern text-editions, including Nestle, deviate from the textus receptus. It would be advisable to offer a textual commentary with this new edition. This commentary could indicate at what points the textus receptus may be labelled as a deviation from the Byzantine text and at what points different readings occur within the Byzantine tradition itself[102].

[100] *The New Testament in the Original Greek according to the Text followed in the Authorised Version together with the Variations adopted in the Revised Version*, edited by F.H.A. Scrivener. Cambridge 1894, ²1902.

[101] Compare note 5.

[102] Cf. the manner in which the textual testimony of the lectionaria for some sections from James is described by K. Junack, Zu den griechischen Lektionaren und ihrer Überlieferung der katholischen Briefe (in: K. Aland [ed.], *Die alten Übersetzungen des Neuen Testaments, die Kirchenväterzitate und Lektionare*. [Arbeiten zur neutestamentlichen Textforschung.] Berlin 1972, pp. 498-591, esp. 553-569; 576-589).

The indication of these different readings can take place even before the number of witnesses for each individual variant reading has been completely determined. It will be a laborious and costly undertaking to determine that number and to provide a complete textual critical apparatus with the traditional text. One could consider whether it is not possible to determine the weight of variant readings in this traditional text in more detail, only in those cases in which the variant reading can be relevant for translation and exegesis. The number of such variant readings is only a small section of the total orthographical, lexical, syntactical or grammatical variations.

There is plenty of work for Reformed textual criticism. She, however, directs her attention to defining a conviction and does not lose herself, like the modern textual criticism, in a quest for the unknown. How many people will still wish to present themselves in the 20th century for this work on the preservation of the text of the New Testament? How many will still have interest in this work? This question can not easily be answered by people. We can only conclude with the absolute certainty, that the ancient text of God's inspired Word both now and in the future will remain an object of God's special care. This certainty creates for us the obligation to treat the text that has been handed down to us with great care. This obligation lies in the confession of the Reformation (Westminster-Confession chapter 1, 8):

> "The Old Testament in Hebrew (which was the native Language of the People of God of old), and the New Testament in Greek (which at the time of writing of it was most generally known to the Nations), being immediately, inspired by God, *and by his singular Care and Providence kept pure in all Ages*, are therefore authentical: so as in all Controversies of Religion, the Church is finally to appeal into them."